Raven

Raven

XIAN

Charleston, SC
www.PalmettoPublishing.com

Raven
Copyright © 2022 by Xian

First Edition

Paperback: 979-8-88590-600-5

Table of Contents

The Raven Flies

She ran through the double doors of her glass house never to
    look back.
She ran barefoot into the woods.
The red nail polish was left as evidence, like the scene of a
    crime.
Raven, black bird in the sky, shall be painted in red.
We know you're not forgotten, out here alone.
Her name shall not be forgotten.
Her face shall not be forgotten.
For if so,
We shall all fade into the dark.
Raven, black bird come alive, painted red,
You are brought back to life.
You can come out from your disguise.
The night was blind.
She found her way back home, In the glass house she lays
Feet rested, enough running.
Raven, black bird that is painted red,
You shall soar above your people,
Keeping a close eye.
Her bones are crushed, laying in the glass room in the glass
    house.
Her shadow is on its way, what lies on the other side.
She can feel it changing her.
She steps into the light; she will be remembered here,
Every last breath until there's nothing left.
Red raven, soar above your people.

What Built the Raven

There's never enough space in this mind to correctly place
these wild thoughts.

Showing true emotion is what the face does, but when the
mouth speaks, it'll make you feel   different.

Secrets and lies are what built this body, given from both
parties.

These muscles are built strong but still get knocked down and
knocked over.

These eyes are focused but still sometimes wander.

Fingers that reach for the sky and still manage to grab the sun
and the clouds all at once.

The feet that hold everything up and steady, like a boat, take
every step with caution, pride, strength, and purpose, and
despite the secrets and lies, the knocked-down muscles,
this body still has the willingness to go.

This body belongs to the raven.

Sincerely, Your Daughter the Warrior.

There's a fire in between being alive and living.
I cannot tell the difference;
Like a child I am blind to what's right in front of me,
Like a child I am daring but fear everything.
My mother's prayers were clear:
"I pray my daughter finds her way to the young woman I
    know she can be."
I did everything except that, you see; I am not a child
    anymore. I can see everything, even   without my glasses.
My mother gave birth to a fighter, and in her name, that is
    what I will be.

Finally, at Peace.

A white sheet of snow lay tightly over the ground.
You no longer see birds chirping, butterflies flying, or even
people walking.
Is this a dream? I asked myself this question maybe once or
twice.
The ice of the snow, melted under my toes like ice cream, was
left to sit out during a heat wave   in Texas.
My fingertips gladly catch snowflakes, each one with a visible
different pattern.
Is this a dream? I asked myself once more.
I wouldn't mind if it was, because now I can finally have
peace; I can rest my body at peace.

Her.

You undress me with your eyes like nobody's watching.
You kiss me with such pleasure and make love to me with
  passion.
I crave your body when you are gone.
Your touch, your taste, the way you inject my mind with such
  intelligent ways.
You are hard to forget.
No matter how hard I scrub my body, I can still feel your
  touch.
I can still taste your tongue on mine.
You are somebody that I am never going to forget.
Let us live forever.

Soft, Yellow Butterfly.

It's the first day of my last life,
And I can't stop thinking about the soft, yellow butterfly.
His wings glowed like fresh sunlight
When the whole world is covered in a white blanket.
His flap and flutter are very much different but very much the
    same.
The details on his wings he wears on his chest,
Right where his heart sleeps.
This soft, yellow butterfly is gone for now,
But he will find his way back.
Because this is the first day of my last life.

First Born.

It's growing inside her
Like a flower growing in a garden.
Something so small and precious
Shall grow and turn into something so beautiful.
But for now
It will remain
A flower in a beautiful garden.

Tall Tales of the Young.

Getting dressed for the first grade—tan skirt, blue polo, and
   a pink backpack filled with crayons,   books, pencils, and
   everything a first grader needs to survive the first day.
Goodbye kisses at the door, waves at the bus stop. Mother
   leaves tears behind as she rushes back   to the house so she
   can set off on her work day.
A drunk "father" passed out on the sofa with what seems
   like three-day-old beer stains on his   shirt from Friday
   morning.

Burning bacon, smashed eggs, shattered plates, and spilled
   milk. All signs of a broken home.
A lonely mother, a barefoot baby, and a stranger living among
   them.
"We live in a mad world, baby."
There is a message, no feathers, no bone.
You are not forgotten out there alone.
Nights are long. I might fade until I'm gone. Just remember
   the message, baby.

When trouble comes to town, and men like me come around
   you, shoot.
At five years old, I learned this was my right as a female.
He taught me to shoot, not to cry.
Placed my right hand on the rifle.
My daddy warned me about men like you. Don't play me like
   a fool, I will shoot.

Evil Side of Love.

There's not a single person in this world that I crave more
than him.

When we first met, everything was fantastic, everything
started falling into place: new house,   new car, my sweet
baby girl.

I want him to want me so bad that it hurts.

This divorce is just like a break. I will have my knight in
shining armor, even if I have to kill him and keep his
body to myself.

The Two of Us.

I have to pull the lump out of my throat just to speak.
This hasn't been easy for a while.
For neither of us.
But just like the sun and the moon,
We will continue to chase each other,
Around and around in circles we will go.

Betrayal.

You had me convinced my body belonged on a pole.
You told my mom you could make a profit, and she listened.
You had me convinced if I stood quiet and closed my eyes
    that it would be over quickly.
It never was "quick."
I felt every pinch, grab, and touch.
I used to beg my mother to not let you near me,
But the only response I got was,
 "Listen to Daddy. He will buy you ice cream if you behave."

I Am Drunk

I am drunk. I am writing this because I am drunk.
I could have loved her, but I chose to love the bottle first.
She yelled, and I threw the first punch.
Shocked at what I did, as I've never done this before.
I watched her bleed on the floor that our child had once
    crawled upon.
The tiny feet that once pitter-pattered across this floor are
    no more.
The baby shoes that have gone to waste, the white onesies
    that have turned yellow.
And on the floor, the mother still sat, bleeding.

I am drunk. I am writing this because I am drunk.
I could have loved her, but I chose to love the bottle first.
She threw a knife, and I pulled a trigger.
I stood over her body as her children watched.
She was stiff, and cold. She died with her eyes open, and
    unhappy.
Afraid to tell her children what Papa has become.
Young lives assigned to different foster homes.
In and out of juvenile detention centers.
Soon to become like their mother's killer.

I am drunk. I have written this once or twice before, but this
    is different.
There's a better me trapped inside me.
No soul to be found, just the rotting smell of Jack Daniel's
    and the tears of mothers.

I once loved a hamster, but I killed that too. Like Michael
    Myers, I took a knife to its throat.
I'm starting to think that there is no hope for me.
I am drunk, and I love the bottle. I am going to die when I
    have sipped the last sip of this Jack   Daniel's.

I Am Not the One.

You say I am weak, brain-dead, useless.
You shut me down with what you call "words of wisdom."
There is an anchor in you, a pit in your stomach
That was once filled by your mother.
Did that anchor dig deeper, did that pit in your stomach
Growing larger when she died?
If so, don't you dare take your pain out on me.
Don't you dare whip your tears onto my shirt.
And don't you dare spill my coffee just because part of your
    life is shitty.
I have nothing to do with that.
Give your hell to someone else.
Because I am not the one.

Bad on the Bottle.

Vodka, rum, and whiskey were my best friends.

I'm screwed blue and covered in tattoos.

I'm bad on the bottle.

That didn't stop me from taking another shot and bringing
the bottle to the tub that was filled   with cold water.

I sat there, dressed for the club, makeup running, but this is
my happy place.

This could be my last light.

The water seems to be rising, or am I just drowning?

It doesn't matter anyway.

I tell myself more lies as I take another gulp of the rum; it
drips down my chin and into the   water.

The brown drop of rum slips off my lip and splashes into the
water; it immediately disappears,   just like me.

It warmed my heart so comfortably I could pass out in this
tub.

But then that'll be a waste of a good bottle of rum, so I'll
finish the bottle first.

There's no one here to find me until the sun rises.

I'm screwed blue and covered in tattoos, and this is my last
light.

A War Unforgotten.

i am dead. i know i am dead because i feel nothing.
i have a Heart but no heartbeat.
i lay awake in bed at night and
dream of the taste of jack daniEl's
and the warmth it gave me before
i put a bullet in her brain.
her blood spLattered from the
back of her head and onto the kitchen walls.
breakfast was burnt, Plates were broken,
and the money from her wallet sat in
my pocket, soaked from jack daniel's.
they still don't know my naMe,
but in the end, we all die the same.
i just hopE mine is worth a bottle of jack.
i lay awake in bed at night and dream of the
bitter taste of henny and the
unfiltered actions it gave me
as i pulled the kItchen knife from my
wife's stomach.
i hurt her because she Made it easy.
there was no fIght.
i would lie and say her absence is killing me,
but i've already Said my goodbyes to her and the boy.
aware that the child will be like his mother's killer,
i stood back from her body and smiled at my son.
i am a proud faTher.
I lay in bed, absent but still here.
i realized i was far from home, pLunged into the darkness.

i have made new friends with the monsters who hoLd the key
     to my sanity.
i have stood over tHese women's bodiEs
as life itself disappeaRed from their eyes.
they fed my flame, shuffled the cards to
my game and stood quiet when I played my acE.
i have started a war, and i'm prepared to lose it.
but i'll do it with a bottle of jack daniel's and with the
jack rotting in my soul.

Disoriented.

How do you explain to someone that you're not "there"?
You are not the person they say.
You are not you.
How do you explain to someone "when I look in the mirror, I
   don't see anything"?
How do you word that to people who might not understand
   what's going on in your brain?
I sat in the bathroom,
Looked into the mirror at my own reflection,
And saw absolutely nothing.
Now tell me,
How am I supposed to explain that?

Soul Mate.

Just as soon as I thought everything
Was starting to fall apart, I met you.
A soft breeze in the dead of winter,
A yellow butterfly chasing a white, cold snowflake.
You were endless; your love, your time, your passion
Are endless.
You were a complete surprise, an honest,
Sweet, and sour surprise. You were my Sour Patch Kid,
And that's something that I, myself, enjoyed.
We were like moths to a flame, an unstoppable attraction.
You set a fire in me, something that I longed for,
Looked for in other people,
And this whole time you were my key.
And now, I hope that I am yours.

Destruction Is Beautiful.

Some destruction is beautiful.
But I owe myself something too.
There are some things I just want to do for myself.
Yet I never seem to care who gets hurt.

Let It Go.

I woke up today and I realized I am no longer hurt, or upset, or angry. Not because of what happened yesterday or what's going to happen tomorrow, but because there are so many reasons to be happy, to let go of the hurt. Smile because you are alive, because every morning you get a chance to go outside and breathe the fresh, crisp morning air. Smile because the boy you love will always be there no matter how hard it gets. Smile because you've had way more bad days than good days, because those bad days aren't your enemies; they are teaching you lessons and showing you how to overcome being sad, upset, or angry.

Smile because you made it through another day and you're at peace with yourself.

It Girl.

Say her name. You like the way it tastes.
She leaves a trace of red. It used to be your favorite.
You feel out of place, far from home.
It's the beginning of the end.

Reckless behavior, standing in the fire,
You just want to watch the world burn.

Never to be seen again, your shadow leaves a trace.
Her taste runs thick. It leaves a stain.
You're so far from home.

Out here in the darkness, you're lost without her.
Reckless behavior is what she smells,
Stained on you like the day-before liquor.

Standing in the fire, without her your world will burn.
She was your poison; she was your evil.
Leaving red on your lips, you like the way it tastes.

Fade into the dark, drowning in the river.
The world isn't crashing down; you are
So far from home.

She left a trace of red. It used to be your favorite.
She smelled reckless behavior like day-before liquor.
You played with fire, like you played with her.

Reckless behavior, standing in the fire.
You just want to watch the world burn.
Without her you are lost.
So far from home.

The House.

Many houses hold secrets, locked doors hide lies, and wall paint covers the screams of a mother who is on her knees begging God to take the pain away.

The hole in the wall tells a story about a father, a husband, a "man" who doesn't get what he wants and throws a fit. Instead of a fit, he throws his wife, a mother, a lover, through the wall, leaving pieces of Sheetrock, dust, and paint chips in her hair.

Mother to one, soon to another, wife, and lover, doesn't know the difference between love and abuse. She plants in her mind "he loves me" over and over again. Not realizing, she is showing her daughter, firstborn, that this, is what "love" looks like.

The little girl, so small, so fresh to the world, she only knows love, but she doesn't know how stupid it can make you. People had told her many times "I love you" over and over again, but this love that she is seeing from a father that once told her "I love you" is not like the love he is showing her mother. No, this is "I hate you" love, this is "I just want to fuck you" love, this is "I'm going to implant my seed in your uterus and leave" type of love.

And that's exactly what he did. The bigger her belly got, the harder the punches were.

The mother of two, a lover and a soon-to-be ex-wife, started to wake up from a dream she thought was sweet. And with a swing of a wok big enough for two chickens, she began to fight back. She was showing her little girl this, this is what it looks like to fight your enemies, because he was no longer a lover nor a father of two. The mother of two, the lover, the bones, and the fighter to her now new family picked up her kids and started to walk away, closing the door that held back the enemy that was once the "lover, husband, father." And this time around, she was smart enough to separate love from abuse.

Losing Him

I cried because he was gone, because he was alive.
I cried because that bitch had won. She opened
A battle that leads to a war. And I will have my fight.
He had raised me, but I wasn't his seed.
I was a child.
For the first time in my life, I had understood the
True meaning of love and that no one knows how to properly
    give it.
My father was my first heartbreak.
Ripped it right out of my chest.
My mother cried for years, and my brother, a baby
I held in my arms, just sat there, playing.
No one knows the true meaning of pain until your whole
    world
Is ripped right from under your feet and you
start falling at one hundred miles per hour.
True pain is what I felt.
The day
My father
Died.

Marylin Monroe.

She is reborn,
Something fresh for the world to gobble up.
She is new,
Something for the fellows to feast their eyes on.
Her scent lingers in everyone's mouth.
Like a piece of cake, when you
Have her you want to eat it too.
She is bold, something that sticks
And stones can't even knock down.
She is the lover of all lovers, except your lover.

Hurtless.

Tell yourself the truth,
Over and over again, until it's embedded in your brain.
It'll hurt, but that'll be one less hurt you have to worry about.

From Lovers to Strangers.

I'm crying for him.

I'm losing everyone that I love.

Maybe in another lifetime, things will be different.

But that's just it, another lifetime. Decades from now we will be strangers all over again with the   blurriest memories of each other. Passing each other in public and not remembering is something I fear the most.

This feeling of happiness, pain, love, faith, and trust will be gone with the wind; every day that passes will be different.

New people will confront you, and you will act on your natural instinct.

Something I fear the most is losing the one person that I love more than myself, because we might not have had decades. Only today.

Killer.

His blade pressed against my throat.
"Go ahead, kill me. Add another
Ghost to your list.
Another ghost to haunt you."

Reality of Love.

It's easy to fall in love.
It's harder to bring yourself
To the reality that it's one-sided love.
It's easy to want to see the rest of your life
With that one person.
It is harder to actually reach that goal.
You're not going to have all good days,
And all your days aren't going to be bad.
But the reward that's waiting at the end of the tunnel
Is well worth the fight.

We Are as We Are.

We were cold, no shelter, no food, no place to rest our heads at night. We didn't know when and where our next meal was coming from.

We walked the streets as the only objective in our everyday life, looking for a car to hop into, then right out with a quick ten or twenty dollars in our hand.

We have been raped, taken for granted, a gun put to our heads.

We never asked to be put on the streets. Some of us had taken the wrong road one too many times, got with the wrong kind of people who filled our head with nonsense: "Do this, it'll make you feel good." It did, but what happens when that "feel good" goes away?

Some of us have kids or are carrying a child with us. Some of our children are affected by our addiction.

We were not the only ones out here who had it bad. There are many of us all at once trying to get some food; then off to whatever "job" that we had. We all lived together, all together like a big, happy family. Most of us were strangers to one another, family

members to others, and just friends to most. We lived like a pack of mice: wherever one went, the other followed. It wasn't the best living environment, but we made it what it is today.

We didn't know the words "no" or "slow down." We never even took the time to think "this can kill me!" The only feelings that we had in our body was that it made us feel calm. It was like medicine, our drug that made us show the better side of us. We used so much that the veins in our arms couldn't handle it anymore, so we injected each other in our necks. Taking turns with different people and different needles. With no one there to help stop us, it became a habit. We did it every morning and every night.

We were only six, seven, and five, watching our parents hurt themselves. "It's better for me," they told us. We didn't live in a stable home or have stable parents. Every day we would see someone buying, using, or selling. "Will they ever learn the word 'no'?" we asked. We asked so many questions that no one had the answers to.

Positivity Is Everything.

Keep your eyes open. What's in front of you is invisible for
   now, but it will show itself when the time is right.
Keep your heart pure. There's someone out there that wants
   to love you, but right now is not the   right time.
Keep your mind positive. Positivity can open new doors.
Never stop trying to reach past your goal, or someone else will
   snatch it right from your dreams.
Never look back unless it's to see how far you've come.

Dead Girl.

I lay in bed at night,
Awake, of course,
And I feel empty.
I feel stiff as a corpse.
I might as well be dead.
My heart already is.
There's something missing,
And it's you.
I've waited my whole life just
To feel this moment,
But for what?
I'm already dead.
So I lay back down in my
Bed at night, awake,
Of course, and dead as a corpse.

Pit Stop.

You had me convinced my pussy
Was a pit stop for men who needed it.
You had me convinced nobody would love
Me because my mind is strong, and no man
Want's a woman with a mind full of words.
You had me convinced the reason my father
Would sneak into my room at night was because
I was better than my mother.
A five-year-old, better than her mother.

I was convinced my father loved me
When he would cum in my room.
That's what he would always say
When he was finished.
I was convinced I would find somebody
To grow old with if I acted brain-dead.
I was convinced my pit stop would fall apart.
And I hoped it would.

Heartbreak at Its Finest.

I'm lying in bed, and my tears are rolling down my face
    quicker than the Mississippi River.
My heart starts racing like NASA rockets, and my skin begins
    to warm up.
Unaware, I'm silently crying into my pillow so that way the
    sounds of my crying moans won't bounce off the walls
    and rush into my mother's room.
Is this what it feels like? To have your heart
Detached from your veins that pumped blood so fast when
    you were around him?
This is what it feels like when he tells you, without warning,
    that he doesn't want you.
This is a heartbreak at its finest.

About the Author

Xian lives in Philadelphia, Pennsylvania. She loves to read poetry and fiction, which inspires her writing, as well as many other authors from around the world.

Made in the USA
Middletown, DE
28 August 2022

72468735R00027